CAN I TELL
YOU ABOUT
LONELINESS?

CAN I TELL YOU ABOUT?

The "Can I tell you about...?" series offers simple introductions to a range of limiting conditions and other issues that affect our lives. Friendly characters invite readers to learn about their experiences, the challenges they face, and how they would like to be helped and supported. These books serve as excellent starting points for family and classroom discussions.

Other subjects covered in the "Can I tell you about...?" series

ADHD	Gender Diversity
Adoption	ME/Chronic Fatigue
Anxiety	Syndrome
Asperger Syndrome	Multiple Sclerosis
Asthma	OCD
Autism	Parkinson's Disease
Cerebral Palsy	Pathological Demand
Dementia	Avoidance Syndrome
Depression	Peanut Allergy
Diabetes (Type 1)	Selective Mutism
Down Syndrome	Sensory Processing
Dyslexia	Difficulties
Dyspraxia	Stammering/Stuttering
Eating Disorders	Stroke
Eczema	Tourette Syndrome
Epilepsy	

CAN I TELL YOU ABOUT LONELINESS?

A guide for friends, family and professionals

JULIAN STERN
Illustrated by Helen Lees

Jessica Kingsley *Publishers*
London and Philadelphia

First published in 2017
by Jessica Kingsley Publishers
73 Collier Street
London N1 9BE, UK
and
400 Market Street, Suite 400
Philadelphia, PA 19106, USA

www.jkp.com

Library of Congress Cataloging in Publication Data
A CIP catalog record for this book is available from the Library of Congress

British Library Cataloguing in Publication Data
A CIP catalogue record for this book is available from the British Library

ISBN 978 1 78592 243 5
eISBN 978 1 78450 526 4

Printed and bound in Great Britain

ACKNOWLEDGEMENTS

I am hugely grateful for the help of Tina Grant, Andrew James, Ellie Lang, Helen Lees, Dan Norman, Leon Norman, Lily Norman, Louise Redshaw, Diana Senechal, Marie Stern, Heidi Tibbetts, Peter Ward, and all the children and young people who talked about loneliness and solitude for my earlier book on the subject.

CONTENTS

INTRODUCTION

Loneliness is one of the most universal and therefore "normal" emotions, but not many people talk about it – especially to children.

Most people enjoy being on their own sometimes, but this can turn to loneliness. Most people enjoy being with other people sometimes, but this, too, can turn to loneliness. It is good to talk about loneliness, and also about being happily alone and happily with other people. *Can I tell you about Loneliness?* is a guide for children and young people aged 7–13, their families (including siblings, parents/carers, grandparents and wider family), and their teachers and teaching assistants. There are descriptions of school activities and home-based activities that will help with loneliness, including the loneliness experienced in the middle of a crowd. And there are descriptions of how to be alone and happy (what I call "healthy solitude"), because learning how to be alone and happy is a wonderful life skill.

We all go through loneliness at some point, and, like sadness, it is unpleasant but it can be a time when we learn a lot. This book discusses how loneliness is experienced by young people and what we can all do to help.

"Sometimes I get lonely. I want to tell you how it feels.
That's a bit difficult because when you're lonely it's
like you are the only person who feels that way."

"Hello. My name's Jan, and I'm 11. Sometimes I get lonely. I want to tell you how it feels. That's a bit difficult, but I'll try.

I think most of my friends feel lonely sometimes, but they don't talk about it.

Sometimes I'm lonely in school. I'm okay in class, but it can be lonely in between lessons and at lunchtimes. At home, I sometimes feel lonely, especially on Saturdays and during long holidays.

I know my family loves me, and I don't want to sound mean, but when I'm lonely, they can be a bit of a pain. 'Play with your brother!' they say, or 'Help me cook lunch!' I just want to be on my own a bit. I know, it's weird, I'm feeling lonely but don't really want to be with anyone.

I'm told that almost everyone is lonely at some time. But when I feel lonely, it seems like I am the only person who feels that way. And when it stops, it's gone completely and I don't feel it at all. Maybe that's why people don't talk about it much."

"When I feel lonely, I don't like it. And I really know it's loneliness when I feel bad about myself, too."

"Sometimes I enjoy being on my own. I've heard people call that 'solitude'. But sometimes I don't enjoy it, and then I usually feel lonely. When I feel lonely, I don't like it. Loneliness feels different to everything else. It feels sad, as if everyone in the world has someone to love them, everyone except me. When I'm lonely, I feel excluded or shut out.

Sometimes I feel lonely when there are lots of other people around. Then, it's as if everyone is happy except me, and none of them like me.

I can feel lonely even when I know everyone in my family loves me. When I'm feeling lonely, I don't think I deserve to be loved, I guess.

Sometimes I feel lonely when a friend has said they don't want to be with me, after we've argued. Sometimes a group of my friends go off and do something and don't invite me, and that feels the same. Or they unfriend me.

When I'm lonely, it's as if I'm not worth anything, or there's something wrong with me, and that's why nobody wants to be with me. I feel a bit guilty, too. That's how I know it's loneliness – I feel bad about myself. It's not as if I'm depressed or anything: it isn't permanent, it goes away after a while. And when the loneliness goes away, it completely disappears – as if it was never there.

So I sometimes like being on my own in solitude, and I sometimes like being with other people. But loneliness is miserable."

"Sometimes I know that my friends are
fed up with me, or I've argued with them
and I don't have anyone to be with."

"I don't mind school. It can be really good. In class, it's usually okay unless the lessons don't make sense, or we're all messing around. For me, it's the times in between lessons, and sometimes lunchtimes or when we're playing sports, that I feel most lonely in school.

At the end of a lesson, everyone's supposed to be happy to go out and play or something. Usually, I'm happy too. But sometimes I know that my friends are fed up with me, or I've argued with them, and I don't have anyone to be with. Or they are all happy and I'm feeling a bit grumpy. Then, I'll hang around, and a lonely feeling will suddenly appear, like a shiver, and suddenly I don't want to be with anyone. I'll check my shoelaces, or read the notices on the walls, or follow an insect crawling along the ground. But really I'm just lonely.

It happened a lot more when I first started here, but it still happens now.

If one of my real friends comes up and talks to me, the loneliness usually just disappears. But if someone else comes up and says, all nicely, 'Come and play with us,' I'm usually a bit rude to them and carry on being lonely. Maybe they really want to help, but it never seems to feel like that. I just get annoyed and even more lonely."

"It can be a bit of a lonely walk around the school."

"Lunchtime is okay if I'm with some friends, and I love it when we have pasta. But if I'm a bit late in the queue and I sit on my own, I sometimes end up feeling lonely. I don't know why. It's worse if I hate the food – it feels like the food is picking on me.

The days we do sport, if I don't get picked for a team, or if I mess up when I'm in a team and I think everyone is angry with me, I'll suddenly feel lonely. I'll shrink into myself and feel embarrassed. It was worse when I first came here and didn't know people. Some picked on me a bit, too. That doesn't happen much now, but sometimes I still feel a bit lonely.

Oh, and another time I can feel lonely is when I have to leave the class to take a message to someone, or to go to the toilet.

I don't know who else will be about or whether they'll pick on me. So it can be a bit of a lonely walk around the school.

When I fall out with my friends, I'll sometimes get angry, but just as often I'll feel lonely. Teachers can sometimes have the same effect on me. If I don't understand something, the teacher looks so fed up with me, that I feel bad about everything. If there's someone next to me who I can have a joke with, then I won't bother about the teacher so much. But if everyone else seems to understand what's going on, then I sometimes feel lonely. That doesn't often happen. The teachers here are okay. But once or twice, especially in maths lessons, it's not good."

"Sometimes when I'm home early from school and no one is around, I feel as if nobody cares. Or sometimes everyone's busy and they don't want to be interrupted, so they all ignore me. Then, it doesn't feel like it's my home. Just for a moment, I can feel really lonely. Most of the time, my home – and especially my room – is the best place to be, but not when I'm lonely.

It can start even before I get home. Once, my mum was late picking me up after school and it was dark. I knew someone would come, but it started raining and the world didn't seem to like me anymore. I started to feel lonely and it didn't stop all evening.

"The last time I saw my granddad, I thought it
was unfair that he forgot me. When he died,
I realised I could never say 'sorry'. I feel lonely
when I think about how we'll never talk again."

Our family gets on pretty well, and it is our grandparents who keep us all together. So everyone in the family was sad when my granddad died. He was forgetting things for about a year before he died. I think he had dementia. The last time I saw him he didn't seem to know who I was. I know it's mean of me, because he was ill, but I still thought it was unfair that he forgot me. And when he died, I realised I could never say 'sorry'. I feel a bit lonely when I think about how we'll never talk again.

My room's the best place to be. I can go there when I want some peace or to get away from my annoying brother. But I remember last year when my brother went away on a camping trip for a week. I've no idea why, but I was in my room and normally I'd be pleased to be on my own. Instead, I felt really lonely. I guess I must love him after all!"

"When I think about it, the times that I've most often felt lonely are Saturdays and during the long summer holidays.

I usually go out on Saturday – I go to a club in the morning and usually go to a friend's house, or a birthday party or something later. That's good. But when Saturday goes wrong, it can be a really lonely day.

If the club's cancelled, or if there's no one around to visit, I end up at home thinking that the world's empty. Saturdays are supposed to be exciting – not comfy and dull like Sundays. So when nothing much happens, I think I'm missing out on stuff. If I end up watching the television with my mother, I get grumpy and go to my room. But then there's nothing to do, and I feel lonely.

"Saturdays are supposed to be exciting, so
when nothing much happens, I think I'm missing
out on stuff and end up feeling lonely."

The same is true of the summer holidays. The first few days it's 'great – no more school!' Then we go off somewhere, usually to see relatives at the other end of the country. Then, in a good year, we'll fly off somewhere as well. The lonely time, though, is the week or so before going back to school. I'm half thinking about going back to school, and there's nothing to do at home. Well, nothing I haven't done already. I get bored, and then I'll remember something horrible about myself, and then I feel lonely. I wonder if it would be better if the holiday were a couple of weeks shorter?"

"I trust my friends, but things can go wrong.
We argue and say nasty things, and I feel
a mixture of anger and loneliness."

"It's great having friends. They are *my* friends – they are not just part of the school or family. Some friends I've known since I was little. I trust my friends. We all go to the same school and we've been to each other's houses and met each other's families. If I'm feeling lonely I can usually get out of it by talking to one of my friends. We talk about anything, and I feel better straightaway. Or one of them will see that I'm looking a bit miserable and they will come over and have a joke.

I know I get grumpy sometimes, and people being nice to me can make me even grumpier. But my friends let me be myself, even if I am grumpy.

But things can go wrong, too. We can argue, and sometimes say nasty things about each other. It can start as a joke, but then it goes wrong. I feel a mixture of anger and loneliness.

I feel like I don't belong, even if we're all together in the same class. It's strange, being lonely when there are lots of people around, but it happens.

The other difficult time is when I've not seen some friends for a while – like in the long holidays. I lose my confidence and am nervous of contacting them. I think they won't want to see me again, and I end up feeling lonely."

"It feels as if a million people are telling
you that you have no friends. It feels as if
I am not alive. Nothing's worth it."

66 I said before that loneliness is strange –
when it stops, it's gone completely and
you don't feel it at all. So it's hard to say how
loneliness affects me. It feels bad – I know that.
It feels sad, too, when you are being ignored.
You start to think about all the bad things.
Even if it's just a couple of friends ignoring you,
it feels as if a million people are telling you
that you have no friends.

At school, when I'm lonely and with other people I feel as if I can't be myself – because people will judge me. I feel much more sensitive and, to be honest, I don't really like myself when I'm lonely. I feel lost and cut off from people and I'm nervous about doing anything. It's worse if I'm hiding some kind of secret from people.

I worry about myself, and worry about what I do. It feels as if nobody knows who I am, and I don't know myself. It's like I'm not really living, just existing. I feel completely useless.

That's a bit unfair. I know I'm okay. Like I say, I know my family loves me and everything. I even know I'll stop feeling lonely sometime soon. But right in the middle of it, nothing's worth it."

"My dog Bonny likes me, whatever
sort of mood I'm in."

"You probably think I'm really weird, and lonely all the time. I'm not, but I thought I should tell you what it's like. Maybe you feel the same, or maybe it's different. Anyway, I'm only telling you because I think there are some ways that I can help myself feel better when I'm lonely. There are some things that other people do that can help, too. And there's always my dog, Bonny.

Bonny's great. A big old dog, a bit like a Labrador, she's a few months older than me. And she just likes me, whatever sort of mood I'm in. I get to take her out at the weekends, and sometimes when the whole family goes for a long walk she'll tag along with me. Bonny is definitely the best cure for loneliness. She doesn't go 'aw, there, there', which makes me even grumpier. I'm glad dogs don't talk. Bonny just seems to know that I'd probably like to scratch her ears, and then she snuggles up beside me.

I started reading recently. I've been reading for years at school of course. But I got into this series of books – horror-type things – and suddenly it's like I've got the bug. A nice boring Sunday is great for reading. When I'm in the middle of being lonely, I won't talk to people about it. (I sometimes tell Bonny, but that's different.) But I get into a book and I'm taken away to a different place. I'm with the people in the book – really with them, not just reading about them. I can't be lonely there – even when horrible things are happening in the book."

"I like long journeys, in a car or a bus or a train. It feels as if no one is judging me and I can just read or watch something out of the window. I don't know why, but I'm never lonely when I'm travelling like that. It's different if I'm waiting around in a station, but while I'm travelling I see everything flying by without having to make any effort. So there's no room for loneliness.

It's the same when I go on long walks, especially in the countryside, or when I'm climbing hills. Sometimes I go on bike rides, and that's good too. Nobody can get into a conversation when you're riding along, and you just hear the wind whistle past your ears. My friend goes skateboarding and that's probably good as well.

"My room is usually the best place to
be when I'm lonely, especially for the
hour or so before I go to sleep."

My room's usually the best place to be when I'm lonely, and I often go there when I'm in a bad mood. It's funny, because when I was little I used to get sent to my room when I was naughty, but I really enjoyed it. There, I've got my computer games to play and I can relax, especially if I've managed to finish a lot of homework.

Best of all is the hour or so before I go to sleep. Everyone else in the house is busy or already asleep. Nobody bothers me, and no one is shouting at me. For me, it's a calming down hour. I don't need to do anything but close my eyes and sleep."

"Listening to music can cheer me up."

"I like a lot of music, and am always wearing headphones when I can. In my room, I'll play my music loud and have something to drink. Listening to music, I don't have those horrible lonely conversations with myself when I'm telling myself how useless I am. I really listen, and try to learn the words. I like the old music that my granddad liked. They played some from the '70s at his funeral, and I still listen to that. I like listening with headphones because only I can hear it. My own time and my own music. That's a really good way to be on my own.

Music has different moods, and that's good for me. Sad music can cheer me up. Strange, isn't it? Really good, sad music is telling me it's okay to be sad or lonely sometimes. And that helps me feel better. But I'll also play really happy music that's good for dancing to, and I can't help smiling. Music has got lots of emotions in it. It can sing what you're feeling.

I was never very good at painting, but I like drawing – really complicated, detailed, drawings, sometimes copied from books. When I'm drawing, I concentrate really hard on what I'm doing and that means I don't concentrate on my worries. I'm there, on the paper, as if I'm drawing my own escape. Everyone says I stick my tongue out when I'm concentrating, and I'm always like that when I'm drawing.

Quite a few of my friends are into sport. I think they get the same things out of sport that I get from music and drawing. I've never been that good at sport, but I can see why they like it."

"In lessons, I'm not often lonely, but there's a lot that happens that can create loneliness later. The most important thing is that I don't like it when the class messes around. I know teachers don't like it, but my friends don't like it and I don't either. It gives me a headache, and people say things that are hurtful and nasty. I know that I sometimes mess about too, but I'd rather be working – doing work that makes sense and that's a real challenge. I want work that's a bit difficult. Not impossible, but difficult.

"I don't like it when we're allowed to mess around. The best lessons are those I concentrate in and that gives me things to learn, which means I forget about loneliness."

The lessons that are best are the ones where I have to concentrate, like art and when we're reading. Those lessons give me things to think about. That means that I don't get bored and don't have space in my head to get lonely. And if the teachers keep control of the class, then I don't get people saying nasty things about me. The sort of nasty things that get said send me into a bad mood and make it lonely at lunch or in between lessons.

It's good if the teacher gives me things to research in the library or at home. If they give me interesting things to learn, in lessons and outside lessons, that will get me away from loneliness, even if I've got no friends to play with."

"Teachers can give us stuff that we can
disappear into, like drawing. Then we
won't be so lonely outside lessons."

"Teachers can help outside lessons too. I said I like drawing at home, and what started me off was a lesson in school. We were asked to do a 'close observation' drawing of a plant, really zooming in on a simple flower. I lost myself in the drawing. Ever since then I've loved drawing at any time.

I like reading now, too. In English, it would be great to be reading a book that I could choose for myself and I could carry on reading at home. The same goes for music lessons. Let us listen to music we like ourselves, sometimes, and create our own playlists for the lessons.

I'm sure others have their own favourite activities. Teachers just need to work out what they are and give us stuff that we can disappear into. Then we won't be so lonely outside lessons. We'll be thinking about things, or going to the library to read, or asking to carry on drawing after the lesson ends.

More lunchtime clubs and homework clubs would be good too, so we don't have to risk the playground when we've fallen out with our friends, and we don't have to go home to a lonely, empty house.

When I was little, we had a 'forest school', which was just like a corner of the garden with a lot of plants and things. I like going for walks now, so maybe the teachers got me interested. But can't we do things outdoors now we're older? That would blow away the stress of the classroom! Even having a fishtank in the school entrance hall would give us something to look at on our own."

"If grown-ups carry on being themselves, and let me be myself too, I might still end up being lonely but I'll know that I can come out of it."

“ **A** dults can get lonely, too. I was chatting to my auntie last year. She said that before she met her partner she lived on her own and was really lonely. She said she couldn't go to cafés or to the cinema on her own, because she thought everyone would look at her and realise she was lonely. Now, she's much happier – and she says she is happy to go out on her own. It was nice to know that a grown-up could be lonely. Not nice, exactly, but a relief anyway! So if adults talk to me about loneliness, that will help. Brothers and sisters, too.

Grown-ups should learn from Bonny, my dog. Just being around can help, and just leaving me alone, too. Being sweet and kind is nice, but when I'm really lonely, it doesn't do any good. Act normal, not angry ('Why don't you go off and play with your friends!') and not too nice ('You poor thing!' or even worse, 'It'll all be okay in the end!'). Occasionally I suppose I do need to be dragged out of a bad mood – and taken out shopping or to see a relative. But sometimes I just want to be me for a while.

There are lots of great things that happen at home, with all the birthdays and everything. What I'd like is some time after that, to have a break from all the celebrations. That's why I disappear to my room the day after Christmas. It would be good if my family didn't moan at me for doing that!

Basically, carry on being yourselves, and, like Bonny, just let me be myself too. I might still end up being lonely, but I'll know that I can come out of it and no one will tell me off for it."

RECOMMENDED READING, ORGANISATIONS AND WEBSITES

BOOKS AND FILMS FOR CHILDREN AND YOUNG PEOPLE

There are thousands of books for children and young people about aloneness, loneliness and solitude. I've included some here, in alphabetical order by author, but it is a matter of personal taste.

Byrd, R.E. (1995 [1938]) *Alone: The Classic Polar Adventure*. New York: Kodansha.

Admiral Richard Byrd's quite shocking account of his own flight to, and his fight to survive, the Antarctic in 1934. Should be popular with teenagers.

Defoe, D. (2001 [1719]) *Robinson Crusoe*. London: Penguin.

Like Admiral Richard Byrd's book, but based in a hotter climate, and fictional. Based on a real person though – Alexander Selkirk (1676–1721), who was a Scottish sailor marooned for five years on a desert island in the

South Pacific, with the island now called "Robinson Crusoe Island". Popular with readers aged 11 and upwards.

Dickinson, E. (1970) *The Complete Poems*. London: Faber and Faber.

Lots of poems about solitude and loneliness, such as "There is another Loneliness", "The Loneliness One dare not sound", and "I tried to think a lonelier Thing". Popular with teenagers.

Larkin, P. (1988) *Collected Poems*. London: The Marvell Press and Faber and Faber.

Philip Larkin's poems sit alongside those of Emily Dickinson, with more solitude and a less settled loneliness. Good examples are "Best Society" (about how hard it is to achieve solitude), "Counting" (how hard it is to be with someone else), and "Love" (also difficult). But you can hardly read a single poem by Larkin without sensing loneliness. Good for teenagers and older.

McKee, D. (1980) *Not Now, Bernard*. London: Red Fox.

What happens when a child is told to go away by everyone? You get eaten by (or become) a monster. I'm not sure if Bernard is lonely, but he certainly feels rejected and feels bad about that. Children who have felt lonely will read this with relish. Read to children from as young as two.

Morpurgo, M. (1999) *Kensuke's Kingdom.* London: Egmont.

Michael Morpurgo's alternative to *Robinson Crusoe*. A child gets shipwrecked on an island, and it isn't quite the adventure he might have expected, but he is helped by Kensuke, who has his own reasons for being on the island. Beautifully written and suited to children from the age of seven.

Murphy, S. (2009) *Pearl Verses the World.* Somerville, Massachusetts: Candlewick.

Pearl worries because she seems to be in "a group of one" at school. At home she lives with her mother and her grandmother – who has dementia. A sensitive, sweet, touching and tough book for older children and teenagers.

Sendak, M. (1963) *Where the Wild Things Are.* London: Random House.

I'm torn between this and *Not Now, Bernard* as my favourite books for or about aloneness in childhood. This is more realistic (as far as these things go), and has a neater, happier ending but one of my favourite bits in all literature is the wild adventure in the middle of this book. I've never seen a child fail to enjoy it. Read to children from as young as two or three.

Sillitoe, A. (1958) *The Loneliness of the Long-Distance Runner.* London: Star.

This was written for teenagers, so the slang used sounds a bit dated. It is an account of a teenager who gets in trouble with the law and is sent to what would now be called a "young offenders unit" or "juvenile detention centre". He finds solace in cross-country running. When running he is in his own world, and can think for himself – he feels like the first man in the world or, more sadly, the last man in the world, out on his own for an early morning run. I think running is his "cure" for loneliness, and I'd prefer the novel to be called "the solitude of the long-distance runner". But it's a fine account of all kinds of aloneness, including the "honest" and "real" aloneness of the runner. Good for teenagers.

Storr, C. (1958) *Marianne Dreams.* London: Faber and Faber.

A haunting account of a girl who is ill and restricted to her home for a long time after an accident. She finds that drawings she makes before she goes to sleep come alive in her dreams. Like *The Loneliness of the Long-Distance Runner*, it describes intense aloneness and feelings of isolation, and the "escape" into a dreamworld. It was made into a television series (*Escape Into Night*) and a film (*Paperhouse*). I read it myself, aged about ten, and have never forgotten it. Many young people find illness a lonely time – particularly if (as in this book) they feel they are missing out on friendship. (Catherine Storr was at one time married to Anthony Storr, a psychiatrist who himself wrote a valuable and popular book on solitude.)

Tan, S. (2006) *The Arrival*. London: Hodder.

A wordless book of a refugee, wonderful in making the reader understand what it is like to be in a strange land. A man leaves his family to find a better life in another place. He is desperately alone, and the reader may feel he is lonely. Eventually, with the help of strangers, he seems to find a way to live in the new land. Good for age seven upwards.

Thoreau, H.D. (2006 [1854]) *Walden*. New Haven, Connecticut: Yale University Press.

This is Henry David Thoreau's description of the time he spent living on his own in a hut next to Walden Pond (in Concord, Massachusetts). He writes of loneliness and of solitude, and his book is seen as one of the great environmentalist books – as he observes nature so carefully and with such concentration. Any young person who spends time closely observing minibeasts and plants will enjoy elements of *Walden*. Probably for dipping into rather than reading cover to cover, but readers have been re-discovering this as *their* book ever since it was written. For adults as much as for young people.

Yates, R. (2009 [1962]) *Revolutionary Road; The Easter Parade; Eleven Kinds of Loneliness.* New York: Everyman.

Richard Yates wrote a number of novels and short stories. *Eleven Kinds of Loneliness* is made up of eleven short stories of different aspects of loneliness. Two of the stories are based in schools, and "Doctor Jack-o'-lantern" is perhaps the best account of a young person's loneliness that I have read. It is a beautiful and desperately sad tale of a poor, tough, pupil's first few days at school. The teacher makes the "mistake" of befriending him, and he gets his revenge, to everyone's disadvantage. After you've survived the first few weeks of a new school (and not before), you could read this story to understand what it felt like. "Fun with a Stranger", the other school-based story, is more about the loneliness of one of the teachers, but it too would interest a good reader of about 12 and over. Adults will be entranced too.

BOOKS FOR ADULTS

Moustakas, C. and Moustakas, K. (2004) *Loneliness, Creativity & Love: Awakening Meanings in Life.* Bloomington, Indiana: Xlibris.

A father and daughter team of therapists write of childhood and teenage loneliness with great sensitivity. They talk of how feelings of loneliness are usually hidden in childhood – hidden by children, and "covered up" by adults. This can make for more damaging forms of loneliness and anxiety. Instead, if recognised and talked about, loneliness will still be experienced, but it can be a time of contemplation and more healthy solitude.

Rufus, A. (2003) *Party of One: The Loners' Manifesto*. Cambridge, Massachusetts: Da Capo.

Whenever a mass murderer or other evil criminal is caught, someone will say, "Ah, they were a bit of a loner." What's so bad about being a loner? Well, this book is a magnificent manifesto for loners, and all the wonderful, positive creative things done by loners the world over. It is a book to make any loner cheer, and should be read by everyone who is a loner and by everyone who thinks loners are bad or lonely or weird.

Senechal, D. (2012) *Republic of Noise: The Loss of Solitude in Schools and Culture*. Lanham, Maryland: Rowman & Littlefield.

A sensitive account of the need for good solitude, and the relationship between solitude and loneliness, in schools. Diana Senechal is a teacher in New York who avoids all simplistic approaches to the topic and therefore manages to explore the reality of young people's experience of schooling. A wide-ranging and well-written book written by someone who encourages thoughtfulness in and beyond school.

Stern, L.J. (2014) *Loneliness and Solitude in Education: How to Value Individuality and Create an Enstatic School.* Oxford: Peter Lang.

My own book on loneliness and solitude in schools, with significant contributions from children aged seven to eight, and young people aged 12 to 13, as well as adult poets, psychologists, philosophers and adventurers. Asking children and young people about loneliness and solitude transformed my view of the topic. Children as young as seven understood as much about loneliness as any adult I've met. That was sad, but it also encouraged me to write *Can I tell you about Loneliness?* Almost all the children felt lonely sometimes, and all valued solitude. "Enstasy", by the way, is the ability to be comfortable within yourself. It's the opposite of "ecstasy", which means to go out of yourself.

ORGANISATIONS AND WEBSITES

It is difficult to describe organisations dealing with loneliness. Loneliness is not an illness, and shouldn't be treated like one. It is a normal part of life: sad and painful and normal. If a child or young person is constantly lonely, or so lonely that they are feeling suicidal, then of course there are organisations that can help (such as www.childline.org.uk or www.samaritans.org in the UK or school counselling services, local children's advocacy groups and www.childhelp.org in the USA). The first two of these websites, incidentally, also have good accounts of loneliness which children, young people and adults will find helpful. But for the loneliness that almost everyone will suffer, intermittently throughout their lives, the ways of helping are as "normal" as the loneliness is. Sometimes people need actively cheering up, sometimes people need to be left alone; someone who loves you or is your friend can probably work out when to intervene and when to leave alone. And books, activities (like drawing, listening to or playing music, walking) and animal companions are generally the best therapists.

Useful activities for schools and for families include looking at and thinking about pictures depicting loneliness, and music depicting loneliness.

- Using Google images (http://images.google.com), find examples of pictures that might be depicting loneliness. My own examples (used with people as young as seven or eight) are

Picasso's *Tragedia*, Degas's *Dans un café – L'Absinthe*, Lowry's *Three Men and a Cat*, and Caspar David Friedrich's *Woman Before the Rising (or Setting) Sun*. If you attach "thought bubbles" to each of the characters in these pictures, you can ask a child or young person to write in the bubble what the character might be thinking. Then, talk about those thoughts. This activity works well with the young. Adults, though, tend to provide less interesting responses than those of children and young people.

- Using YouTube (www.youtube.com), find examples of music that might be depicting loneliness. My own examples are *Yer Blues* by John Lennon (which is all about loneliness), and *O solitude, my sweetest choice* by Henry Purcell (which is about a very sad form of solitude). A young person who likes music might put together a playlist of lonely music – either music *about* loneliness, or music that would be good to listen to when you are *feeling* lonely.